Disclaimer: the information provided in this guide to readers has been prepared solely for informational purposes and should not be construed as an offer to buy or sell or a solicitation of an offer to buy or sell any security or instrument or to participate in any transaction or trading activity. The author accepts no liability with regard to the user's reliance on it. This guide and the information contained herein are not intended to be a source of advice or credit analysis with respect to the material presented.

Copyright: All rights reserved. No part of this publication may be reproduced, distributed, or transmitted in any form or by any means, including photocopying, recording, or other electronic or mechanical methods, without the prior written permission of the publisher, except in the case of brief quotations embodied in critical reviews and certain other noncommercial uses permitted by copyright law.

Table of Contents

CHAPTER 1. THE POWER OF ACCOUNTING   5

GAAP Principles   6

CHAPTER 2. DOUBLE-ENTRY SYSTEM   10

T-Accounts: The Foundation   11
Journal Entry: The Double Faced Entry   11
Accounts And Chart Of Accounts (COA)   12
How To Record Journal Entries   16
Cash vs. Accrual   17
The General Ledger   19

CHAPTER 3. THE ACCOUNTING WHEEL   20

The Angry Boss   20

CHAPTER 4. A BRIEF OVERVIEW OF THE MAIN FINANCIAL STATEMENTS   26

Introduction To The Main Financial Statements   26
Income Statement (P&L): Show me The Bottom Line   28
Balance Sheet: The Power Of The Now   29
Cash Flow Statement (CFS): Cash Is King   29
Real Life Analogy   30

CHAPTER 5. THE INCOME STATEMENT — 30

REVENUE — **33**
EXPENSE — 36
NET PROFIT: GET READY FOR A SHOCKING TRUTH — **40**

CHAPTER 6. THE BALANCE SHEET — 42

A SIMPLE EQUATION: ASSETS = LIABILITIES + EQUITY — **44**

ASSETS: THE FUTURE OF THE BUSINESS — 50
CURRENT ASSETS — **53**
NON-CURRENT OR LONG-TERM FIXED ASSETS — 59
LIABILITIES: TOO MUCH OF IT CAN GET YOU IN TROUBLE — **68**
EQUITY: STRIKE THE RIGHT BALANCE — **72**
BALANCING THE BOOKS — **76**

CHAPTER 7. THE CASH FLOW STATEMENT — 77

CASH IS KING — **78**
THE THREE MAIN SOURCES OF CASH — 81
CASH INFLOW VERSUS CASH OUTFLOW — 84
THE NET PROFIT IS A LIAR — **86**
CASH FLOW FROM OPERATIONS: ARE WE EFFICIENT? — **88**
CASH FLOW FROM INVESTING: ARE WE KILLING THE GOOSE? — **95**
CASH FLOW FROM FINANCING: THE CASH PARADOX — **98**

BOOK CONCLUSIONS 103

ABOUT THE AUTHOR 106

ONLINE COURSES 107

ADDITIONAL SUGGESTED READING 108

USEFUL WEBSITES 108

Chapter 1. The Power Of Accounting

In a globalized world, where change happens so quickly that companies that existed for centuries (such as Lehman Brothers, founded in 1850, bankrupted in 2008) just few things stick for centuries.

The current accounting system is one of the few survivors. Born in 1494, when a Venetian Merchant, Luca Pacioli, in his "Summa de Arithmetica, Geometria, Proportioni et Proportionailta," described for the first time the double entry-system. This practical manual gave official birth to a system that is still used in current accounting.

Even people who hate accounting recognize the importance of it. If you either own a small business, or you are a CFO, CEO, COO, a common citizen, you have to understand accounting to recognize what is behind each one of the 14 trillions transactions per day, just in US·

GAAP Principles

Although, the fundamental accounting system hasn't changed, the principle and rules applying today have been updated in the last century.

The general accepted accounting principles are standards and procedures used by organizations to submit their financial statements. Today we have two main accepted frameworks, globally: GAAP and IFRS; in this chapter I will focus mainly on GAAP. Indeed, after the 1929 market crash, American government felt the necessity to create a set of rules to discipline and conform the accounting system, and avoid what had happened. In the decade after the 1929 market crash institutions such as the Securities and Exchange Commission were created. In 1934, the SEC, assisted by the American Institute of Accountants (AIA), started to work on the GAAP. The AIA subsequently instituted an organism to specifically create these principles: The Committee on Accounting Procedure (CAP).

Finally, the first set of GAAP was created and in 1973 and the CAP board was substituted by the Financial Accounting Standards Board (FASB). From this work came out 10 basic principles, that are the foundation of the modern accounting system in US:

- *Economic entity assumption:* If you have a business, even if you are a sole proprietor, the accountant will consider yourself separately from your business.
- *Monetary Unit Assumption:* The Business activity you undertake is considered in US Dollars.
- *Time Period Assumption:* Business activity you undertake can be reported in separated time intervals, such as weeks, months, quarters or fiscal years.
- *Cost Principle:* If you buy an item in 1980 at $100, it will be reported on your balance sheet as worth $100 today, independently on inflation or appreciation of the asset.
- *Full Disclosure Principle:* You have to report all the relevant information of the

business in the financial statements or in the footnotes.

- *Going Concern:* The accountant assumes that your business will continue its operations in the foreseeable future.

- *Matching Principle:* If you incur an expense, it should be matched with the revenues, according to the accrual principle. If you decide to pay your employees a bonus related to 2015 but you pay it in 2016, you still will report it as 2015. You will report the expense when it was recognized and not when actual cash was disbursed (accrual principle).

- *Revenue Recognition Principle:* if you sell a product in January 2015 but you will receive the money from the customer in April 2015, you will report the sale in January, since it was the period when the actual sale was realized.

- *Materiality Principle:* when you report the financials, it will be allowed to round them, since if an amount is insignificant can be neglected by your accountant.

- *Conservatism Principle:* When in doubt between $80 and $100 loss, your accountant has to choose the most conservative alternative, report $100.

These principles are the "ten commandments" for the accountant. Keep them in mind. They will guide you throughout the book. In addition, the accrual principle in practical terms states: *"Revenues and expenses are recognized when occurred, independently from cash disbursement."*

This principle is crucial to build our main financial statements, in particular the Income Statement and Balance Sheet.

Chapter 2. Double-Entry System

As any other language, the accounting system has its own. Indeed, in accounting in order for you to record a transaction you have to use the double-entry system. Double-entry means that each single transaction needs to be recorded twice, on the left side if debited and on the right side if credited. Usually, when you think of debit or credit in real life is different compared to debit or credit in accounting. In fact, debit does not mean that you have a debt to be paid back; neither credit means that you have money to receive.

For example, in the accounting world, when cash is debited, it means the cash on your bank account increased. Therefore, you received cash. I know it may sound counterintuitive, but this system was created five hundred years ago and it is the system today's accountants use to record each single transactions.

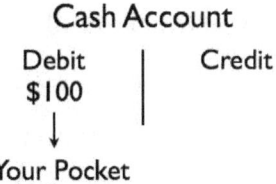

T-Accounts: The Foundation

The most effective way that accountants use to record each single transaction in the ledger is the T-Account. Although, most of the accounting Software today do it automatically, it is helpful to know how it works.

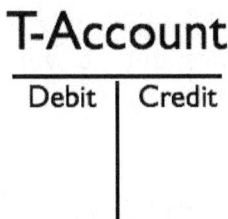

This visual aid helps the accountant to record a single transaction. Each account, in fact, has two sides, debit and credit. Therefore, for a transaction to satisfy the accounting requirements has to be recorded on both sides. We will see that in the next paragraph.

Eventually, all the transactions collected for a certain period flow in the General Ledger.

Journal Entry: The Double Faced Entry

Assuming you own a bakery that just sold $100 worth of biscuits. In the real world, it appears as a single transaction. Therefore you may think the same applies in the accounting world. Instead, it is more complex since each single transaction implies two concurrent movements. When you sold $100 of biscuits, your customer paid in cash. It means, on one hand, the $100 is debited to the cash account, while on the other hand, the $100 is credited to the income account. It will look like the following:

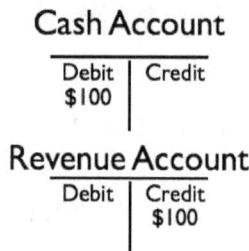

Accounts And Chart Of Accounts (COA)

By defining Accounting as the language, we can define the accounts as the letters of the alphabet. Indeed, the accounts allow to categorize the bunch of transactions happened in a certain period, under the same umbrella. The account is a record where all the debit and credit transactions are recorded. In the previous paragraph you saw already two of the main accounts, Assets and Revenue. These accounts get organized under a Chart of Account (COA) or a list of items identified by an organization that will flow in the General Ledger (GL). This will help the company to build reports such as: Balance Sheet (BS), Income Statement (P&L) and Cash Flow Statement. Setting up a clear and consistent COA is crucial for the accounting department internal organization. Indeed, a disorganized COA can lead to many accounting mistakes and inaccuracies. Below an example of best practice:

Accounts numbering
- 1000 - 1999: asset accounts
- 2000 - 2999: liability accounts
- 3000 - 3999: equity accounts
- 4000 - 4999: revenue accounts
- 5000 - 5999: cost of goods sold
- 6000 - 6999: expense accounts
- 7000 - 7999: other revenue (for example, interest income)
- 8000 - 8999: other expense (for example, income taxes)

By separating each account by several numbers, many new accounts can be added between any two while maintaining the logical order.
Mycrosoft Dynamics template

As you can see, it is suggested to use four figures. In the specific example, each account has its own range. Indeed, the assets are shown under 1xxx, liability 2xxx, equity 3xxx and so on. It is advisable, when setting up the accounts to leave some space between the sub-accounts. For example, under assets we have the sub-heading "current-assets." Within the Current Assets, we have items such as: Cash Account, Accounts Receivable, Inventories and Prepaid Expenses. Therefore, we will have: Current Assets, 1100 code; Cash Account, 1110 code; Accounts receivable 1200 code; Inventory 1300; Pre-paid Expenses 1500 code. Give space between the sub-accounts, this allows you to set up new sub-accounts when needed. For example, if two new cash accounts are opened, you can use the coding from 1111-1199. Therefore, you have plenty of space to organize your COA. Setting up an organized COA and making sure everyone follows it rigorously in the organization is crucial. Indeed, according to the codes generated, all the internal reports will be built. Such as historical AR, AP, P&L, BS, GL, CFS. If the coding is wrong or disorganized so your reports will be.

The main accounts are:

- *Assets:* Resources owned by an organization. They will produce future benefits for the company. For example, you own a bakery that has to produce biscuits. In order for you to produce them, you have to buy a machine. The machine will be an asset for your organization.
- *Liabilities:* Obligations (Debt) contracted by an organization. Your bakery

bought $100 of raw material from the supplier and you will pay in 60 days. Until the payment will be made the $100 will show as liability (future debt) on your balance sheet.

• *Owner's Equity:* Amount of money or resources you endowed to your organization. The accounting definition is: Owner's Equity = Assets – Liabilities.

• *Revenue or Income:* The $ amount of sales occurred in a certain period. According to the accrual principle, income is recognized independently from cash receipt.

• *Expenses:* The $ amount of costs occurred in a certain period. According to the accrual principle, expenses are recognized independently from cash disbursement.

How To Record Journal Entries

Let me show you now a table that will help you with the recording or journal entries related to the single accounts. Indeed, Assets have different sets of rules compared to liabilities when it comes to the debit and credit (double entry) system.

	Debit	Credit
Asset	Increase	Decrease
Liability	Decrease	Increase
Income	Decrease	Increase
Expense	Increase	Decrease
Equity/Capital	Decrease	Increase

If you look at the asset, they move in the same sense of the expenses.

Instead, Liabilities, Income and Equity (Investment) move in the opposite direction. We can use a mnemonic technique to recall the table above, such as: "*E*dgar and *A*lan *lie*d". Therefore: "Edgar" (Expense) and "Alan" (Asset) move together, "*Lie*d" (Liabilities + Income + Equity), move together in the opposite direction.

Cash vs. Accrual

In chapter 1, through the matching and revenue recognition principle, we saw that GAAP calls for the accrual principle. Furthermore, while big corporations or listed companies have to report their financials in accrual basis, this is not always true for small businesses that instead can choose between the accrual and the cash basis.

What is the difference between the two?

The former states that revenue/expense must be recognized in the moment in which they occur independently from cash receipt/disbursement. For example, if you buy $50 of raw materials, and your supplier delivers it to you, the expense will be recognized, even though you will pay in 60 days. See the transaction below:

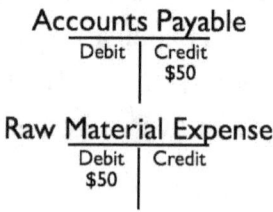

The latter, instead, states that revenue/expense must be recognized when cash is received/disbursed. For example, if you buy $50 of raw materials, the expense will be recognized in the moment your supplier receives the cash from you. See the transaction below:

The General Ledger

It is the centerpiece of the accounting cycle. Indeed, the General Ledger (GL) is an overwhelmingly long and big book where all the transactions related to a certain period are recorded. Today, the GL is automatically generated by accounting software such as QuickBooks and SAP. From the GL all the main financial statement reports are generated. One of the main tasks of the accountants is to keep it as clean as possible. Thus, the accuracy of the GL is crucial for the accuracy of the reports generated.

Chapter 3. The Accounting Wheel

"I just wanted to be a businessman, and for me the best way to understand business was to be an accountant" **Aubrey McClendon** (Credit: BrainyQuote)

The Angry Boss

It may seem a little odd to title this paragraph "The Angry Boss", let me give you an explanation for that. In most of the firms, from IT to Manufacturing, before the financials are given to the CFO, they follow a rigorous internal process. According to the firm size, this process may involve few to dozens people within and outside the accounting department. An accountant knows how rigorous the process is and if any step is missed or not taken properly, this will make the boss very angry. The boss of the bosses within the accounting department is the Controller. Who is the Controller? Let me show you the organizational chart of the accounting department:

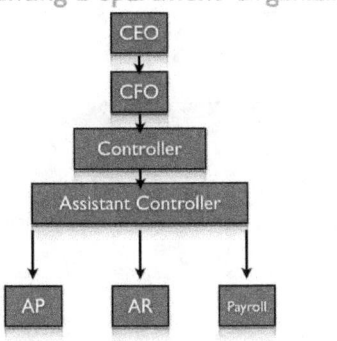

Accounting Department Organization

At the bottom of our pyramid there is the AP (accounts payable specialist), AR (accounts receivable specialist) and Payroll specialist. Once transactions have been collected and recorded in the system Assistant Controller in cooperation with Controller review and close the books. "Closing the books," means locking them up with a special passcode or other systems, to avoid past transactions to be manipulated. Furthermore, the reports generated by the system will be sent to the CFO who will analyze them with help of Financial Analysts. The set of internal procedures within the accounting department take a shape that looks like the "Accounting Wheel" below:

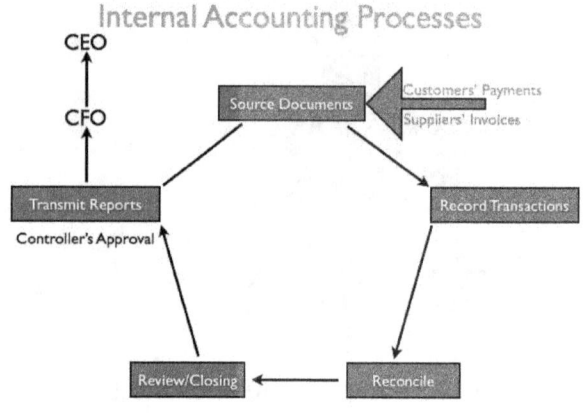

Source Documents – Always have a back up. The accounting process is rigorous and time consuming. It starts with the payments made by customers and invoices generated by suppliers. Before any transaction can be recorded in the system, it needs approval by the manager who received the payment from the customer or the invoice by the supplier. The accountant will ask for documents to supports such transactions. Once these source documents are collected, the accountant will record the transaction in the system. The recording will happen with the same principles you saw in chapter 2 (How to record journal entries).

Reconcile The Books. At this stage, the books need to be reconciled. The reconciliation process happens each month.

Why do you need to reconcile the books?

The purpose of this process is to make sure all the transactions recorded in the accounting system are matching with the cash transactions happened on the company's bank accounts. This phase is crucial, and it implies a lot of hard work for the accountants. Indeed, if any mismatching is found between what recorded in the system and what shown on the bank account it may signal other issues and it needs to be resolved, before the books are closed. Even though most of the accounting processes are automated, this stage is actually very manual. In fact, many times accountants have to check, one by one, all the transactions happened in a certain month and compare it with the Bank Statement issued by the Bank. If something is not reconciling, the accountants after Controller's approval will record "*adjusting entries*" to balance the books again. The adjusting entry works like a journal-entry. It is called "adjusting" because it is entered in special circumstances.

Audit & Close the Books. At this stage of the process, financials (General Ledger, Balance Sheet, Bank Reconciliations, Accounts Receivable, Accounts Payable, Income Statement) and other back up collected by accountants are audited. The auditing phase helps to assess whether the internal procedures have been followed.

Eventually, the Assistant Controller or Controller proceeds with closing the books. Closing is like locking a door to avoid anyone entering again. Indeed, if books were not closed, anyone could go back and change transactions happened in the past, this would damage irreparably your books. In addition, the closing is crucial at the end of the year for tax return purposes.

The Happy CFO: Eventually, the financials are ready for the CFO. After the time consuming job of the accountants directed by the Controller, reports are officially generated. The accounting software delivers the reports to the upper management. Of course, the CFO gives direction to the accountants throughout the whole process. Accountants perform the time consuming part. They must deliver clean and accurate reports to the upper management.

As you saw from this chapter, although management takes such reports fro granted, there is a lot of work going on before they are produced. Indeed, also what would be otherwise considered a minor oversight can have bad consequences on the accounting books (think of when your balance-sheet does not reconcile, you are in trouble also if the amount missing is $1). Therefore, it is crucial to establish a clear and manageable process, where the workflow within and without the accounting organization is continuous.

Keep reading until the end and get the gifts The Four-Week MBA has prepared for you.

Chapter 4. A Brief Overview of The Main Financial Statements

The first part of this text, focused on the accounting cycle and internal processes. In few words you were shown the "how to" that internally leads to the production of financial reports. In the second part of the text, you will be shown the "Why" and "How" of the main financial statements used in reporting and financial accounting. Indeed, even though financial statements are produced for internal management as well, most of the time they are pointed externally.

Introduction To The Main Financial Statements

The main financial statements are: Balance Sheet, Income Statement and Cash Flow Statement. Each of these statements has a different purpose and together they give us specific information in regard to: "*Return, Risk and Cash*".

First, if you look at the income statement, there is no way you would make any assessment about the risk of the organization in that particular point in time or the cash produced in a certain period. Instead, the Income Statement (or Profit & Loss) will show you the **return** generated by the business.

Second, if you want to understand how an organization acquired the resources to operate the business, you have to look at the Balance Sheet. How does the balance sheet assess the **risk** of an organization? Simple: there are two ways a company can acquire resources, either through Equity or Debt. As you can imagine, too much debt can be dangerous. What would occur if you run a business and suddenly your creditors ask for the money you owe them? You would go bankrupt. Instead, when debt in proportion to the equity is dismal, this makes your organization creditworthy and safer.

Third, it happened many times in the financial world history to see profitable companies bankrupted due to a poor cash management. The cash flow statement helps you to answer questions such as: How much cash did we make? Where did the cash come from? In fact, an organization can find cash through three main activities: Operating, Investing and Financing.

INCOME STATEMENT (P&L): SHOW ME THE BOTTOM LINE

The main purpose of the income statement is to show the **return** of the business in a certain period: Quarterly, Biannually or Yearly. The income statement is built around the bottom line, the "*net profit.*" Do not be surprised to notice your eyes unexplainably falling on the net income. In fact, accountants make it as visible as a fluorescent fish ready to mate. This distracts you by other metrics on the Income Statement that are as important as the Net Income.

Balance Sheet: The Power Of The Now

The main purpose of the Balance Sheet is to show the ***risk*** of the business in the particular moment you are looking at it. In Fact, if you look at the balance sheet on January 1st it won't be the same on January 2nd. Of course, this is true for the P&L and CFS (Cash Flow Statement) as well, but the balance sheet is an instant snapshot of the business more than a collage of pictures taken in different moments, like the Income Statement.

Cash Flow Statement (CFS): Cash Is King

The main purpose of the CFS is to show the ***cash*** generated by an organization in a certain period: Quarterly, Biannually or Yearly. It doesn't matter how much profits a business is making, one way to know whether the business will survive in the next future is to look at the cash. Generating cash is not easy task and the organizations who are able to keep their profits stable and generate enough cash to sustain their operations and invest for future growth are the ones who thrive.

Real Life Analogy

Let me use a real life analogy here. If you are a photographer in order for you to do your job, you must have a professional camera. In addition, you can take instant pictures or build a collage of pictures you have taken in the last three months, and remember the camera will work as soon as the battery will be charged. Indeed, you can compare the single picture or "instant picture", at your balance sheet, while the "collage" pictures taken in the last three months, at your P&L. Furthermore, you want to see what's the level of charge of the battery and how long the camera will operate. The battery life can be compared to your CFS. Indeed, a lack of cash for a business is almost like a lack of oxygen for an individual. According to your needs you can look separately at each statement.

However, if you want the whole picture of the business you must look at all of them concurrently.

Chapter 5. The Income Statement

"Numbers have life, they are not just symbols on a piece of paper" **Shakuntala Devi** (Credit: BrainyQuote)

At this stage, you know already, when you look at your P&L, it will answer questions such as:

Is the company making any return?

Is the organization making enough revenues to cover for its expenses?

Let us see a real Income Statement below:

Example, Company XYZ
Income Statement January thru December 31, Year 1

	Year 1
Revenue	6,000
COGS	4,000
Gross Profit	2,000
Advertising	(100)
Salaries and Wages	(600)
Phone and Internet	(34)
Depreciation Expense	-
Office Supplies	(25)
Total Operating Expenses	(759)
Operating Profit	1,241
Interest Expense	(200)
Interest Income	-
Profit Before Tax (EBT)	1,041
Tax	(141)
Net Profit	$900

The Income Statement or Profit and Loss is a financial statement that shows the Profit or Loss incurred by an organization in a certain period of time. In this example we saw the P&L for the year. In addition, this statement can be produced for the year, quarter, month. In regard to reporting purposes, instead, the P&L can be published every three or six months. In the above example the P&L shows the Income as positive and the costs as negative. There are several methods to present the P&L. On one hand, you can use the method where costs are reported already as negative numbers compared with revenues. Indeed, to obtain the Gross Profit (third line), you can simply use the sum() formula in excel:

Revenue	6,000
COGS	(4,000)
Gross Profit	2,000

On the other hand, you can use another method, where all the items are shown with a positive sign and then you just subtract the costs from the revenues to obtain the Gross Profit. See the example below:

Revenue	6,000
COGS	4,000
Gross Profit	2,000

Whether you decide to use the first or second method it is irrelevant, however what matters is consistency. In fact, if you use this method for your income statement you must use it across all the other financial statements you are building, to avoid confusion.

In the following chapter, the accrual principle will be our guiding principle. For Example, prepaid expenses incurred in Year 2, will not appear on the P&L the following year. The same applies to the revenues. If customers paid in advance for service to be rendered, the income will be not recognized until the service will be provided.

The first item of the Income Statement is Revenue. Imagine you have a bakery that sells donuts at $1 each and you sold 100 donuts, your total revenue for the day will be $100. Even though some customers paid with credit cards and the cash on your bank account will be deposited within thirty days you will still recognize $100 in Revenue.

How can we break the Revenue down? See the diagram below:

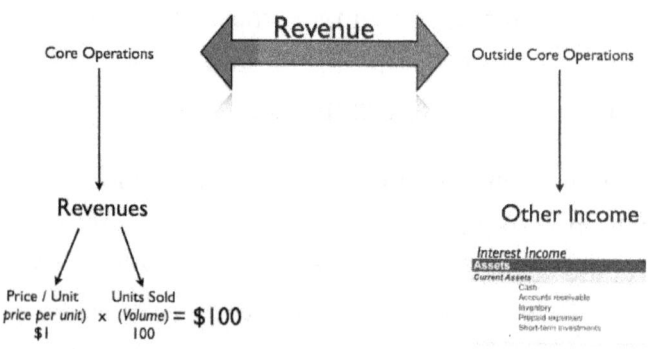

The two main sources of Income are coming from: core business operations or outside core business operations. Furthermore, we can identify the former as Operating and the latter as Non-Operating revenue.

• *Operating Revenue:* They are generated by the sales coming from the core product or service, which the organization produces.
• **Example:** Imagine owning a Pizza Store. The income generated by selling pizzas will be considered Operating Revenue. In the example, the Operating Revenue formula is: price per unit times Units Sold (Volume). Indeed, if the price for your pizza is at $1 per unit, and 100 pizzas were sold, your revenue will be $100.
• *Non-Operating Revenue:* They are generated by sales coming from sources not related to the core business operations.
• **Example:** Imagine your Pizza Store business is going pretty well and you are generating cash in excess that can be invested

in short-term instruments such as bonds. Later, you go to the bank and buy $1,000 of T-Bills. This is a short-term debt obligation backed by U.S. government with a maturity of less than one year. Your T-Bills are due in six months, after that you will receive a simple interest of 2% annually or $10. The $10 you receive after six months is Interest Income or non-operating revenue, also described as incidental or peripheral income. However, on your balance sheet the interest income will be reported after the interest expense, almost like an offsetting. It is more accurate to report the interest income together with the other non-operating expenses. In this way the income generated by interests will not distort our Gross Income. Indeed, the Gross Income is a metric of operational efficiency. See below how to display your interest income:

EXPENSE

The other main component of the income statement is cost/expense. There are many costs incurred by an organization. That is why most of the time can be very tricky to categorize them. In addition, cost categorization is crucial for any business, since they represent a big piece of the pie of any organization's profits. If not managed properly can lead to big issues, ultimately to bankruptcy. In fact, there are several methods that can be used to classify costs, such as: Operating vs. Non-operating, Direct vs. Indirect, Variable vs. Fixed. It all depends by the perspective from which you look at them. Each one of these methodologies has the purpose of better understanding the cost structure of the organization, the so-called "cost accounting." In this chapter we are going to take into account three main categories of costs for reporting purposes:

- Cost of Goods Sold (CoGS)
- Operating Expenses
- Non-Operating Expenses

Cost of Goods Sold (CoGS) is the cost incurred to generate the revenue for the period in consideration. For example, a company who produces Smart Phones will have actual costs of production. These costs, such as: Raw

Materials, Wages associated to manufacturing, Overhead costs of running the factories, will be all considered CoGS. These costs can be defined as direct costs as well. After subtracting CoGS from Revenue we get the Gross Profit. This metric can be pretty useful in assessing the profitability and efficiency of the business when it comes to the manufacturing process. We will see it more in detail in Chapter 7.

Operating Expenses are all the costs not included in the CoGS. These costs are related to the operations of the business, such as: Advertising, salaries and wages, phone and Internet. However, they are not incurred to generate sales or at least in many cases it is hard to track the effect of this cost over the additional sale incurred by the organization. After subtracting the operating expenses from Gross Profit we get the Operating Profit. This metric is useful as well to assess the profitability and efficiency of the business when it comes to the overall operations. We will see it more in detail in *Chapter 8*.

Non-Operating Expenses are the remaining costs not included in the previous categories. They are incurred outside the business operations (non-directly tied to business operations).

Example: Imagine you own a Coffee Shop. Suddenly your sales plunge, you still need money to finance the operations, since the alternative would be closing the business. Therefore, you go to the bank and ask for a short-term loan of $4,000 that will be repaid in six months. The loan will carry a simple interest of 5% annually. Therefore, at the end of the six months, after paying the principle, you will eventually pay for the interest of $100. The money paid as interest will show under the Income Statement as interest expense for that period.

The revenue minus the operating and non-operating expenses for the period, give us the Net Income. This metric is very important to assess the overall efficiency and profitability of the business. We will see it in detail in *Chapter 8*.

Net Profit: Get Ready For a Shocking Truth

Whichever profits are shown on your income statement they do not tell you anything about cash. It might be a shocking truth for who is new to Accounting. Indeed, this is not always true, especially if we operate under the cash basis, instead of the accrual basis principle. On the other hand, remember that according to GAAP standards, the accrual principle is our guide throughout this book. Therefore, we will see it more in details in *Chapter 7*, when you will be shown the cash flow statement. As of now, it is useful for you to understand that in the P&L, because of the accrual principle, the revenue and expense must be only the ones related to the period in consideration.

Example: Imagine you own a bakery that sold $1,000 in chocolate cakes in the first month. This event does not imply that you have $1,000 on your bank account. In fact, most of the time customers pay within 60/90 days. Therefore, half was received in cash; the other half was bought on credit. Thus, the first half ($500) is an actual cash inflow, the other half

($500), instead will be reported on your Balance Sheet. The transaction can be recorded like the following:

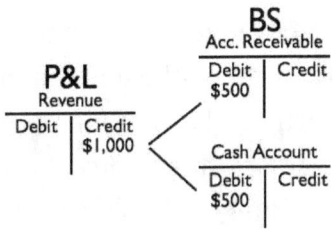

Imagine now, the bakery incurred $500 of expenses in that same period for raw materials; Half is purchased on account, and half paid on account. This implies a cash outflows for $250. The other half will show on the Balance Sheet, under Accounts Payable (Current Liability's Section). See below:

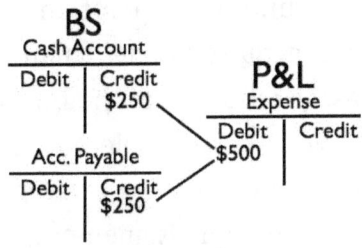

In order for you to know how much cash the company generated, you will combine the information provided by the P&L and adjust it according to the Balance Sheet. In this regard, we could define the P&L as the father and BS as the mother. They give offspring to the Cash Flow. Therefore, through the understanding of Risk and Return cash is generated. It is important to grasp this concept, since it explains many things about the business world.

Chapter 6. The Balance Sheet

Indeed, as we saw in *Chapter 4*, the balance sheet is the other main financial statement used in financial accounting. The purpose of the balance sheet is to report the way the resources to run the operations of the business were acquired. The Balance Sheet helps us to assess the risk of the business. By looking at it you will be able to answer to questions, such as: What is the leverage? Is the company liquid enough? Remember, leverage means the proportion between equity and debt, while liquidity is the capacity of the business to repay for its short-term obligations, to run the operations. While we will answer to these questions in *Chapter 8*, in this chapter we will focus on why the balance sheet is important and how it works.

Example: Imagine you want to open a restaurant. The overhead costs, plus the costs of running the business are $200,000. There are two ways for you to find the money needed to open the business, assuming you don't have the resources to do it your own. Either you find a partner that would put in personal money or you ask for a loan. Therefore, Equity and Debt are the two ways to finance your business. This is how a typical balance sheet looks like:

Assets
- *Current Assets*
  - Cash and Cash Equivalents
  - Short-Term Investments
  - Accounts Receivable
  - Inventories
  - Prepaid Expenses
- *Total Current Assets*
- *Non-Current Assets*
  - Plant & Equipment
  - Licenses & Patents
  - Building
- *Total Non-Current Assets*

Total Assets

Liabilities
- *Current Liabilities*
  - Accounts Payable
  - Accrued Expenses
  - Wages Payable
  - Taxes Payable
- *Non-Current Liabilities*
  - Long-Term Debt
  - Note Payables
- *Total Liabilities*

Equity
- Common Stocks
- Retained Earnings
- Shareholders' Equity
- *Total Equity*

Total Liabilities & Equity

A Simple Equation: Assets = Liabilities + Equity

Before moving on, try to memorize this simple equation, always true: assets have to equal the liabilities plus equity.

Example: Imagine you are starting a company, which manufactures biscuits. Beside the cost to run the operations, you need the machine to produce them. In total, for the machine you need $100,000. The purchase is financed: 80% through equity and 20% through debt. Even though this transaction is one step in the real world, it becomes three steps in the accounting world:

Step 1: Initially your balance sheet will show $80K under cash and equity, since remember that you will contribute 80% of $100K to buy the machine. The transaction will look like the following:

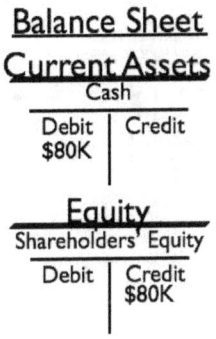

Step 2: Next, you will borrow $20K from the Bank as long-term loan, since 20% will be financed with debt. You will show $100K under cash now ($80K + $20K). On the other side, you will show $80K under equity and $20K under liability. The transaction will look like the following:

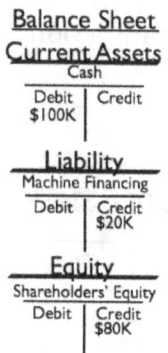

Step 3: With the resources acquired you will buy the machine that will cost you $100K. The machine will show as a long-term asset on the balance sheet. This asset, financed with $20K as a long-term liability and $80K as Equity. See below:

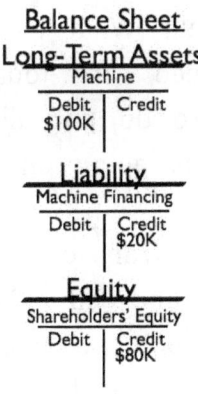

Keep in mind these two principles: First, Assets *always equals* Liabilities + Equity. Second, what is a one step transaction in the real world becomes a three steps transaction in the accounting world. I am sure at this point you are thinking of accounting as of "the art of making easy things hard." Although, I can assure you that once you internalize the two principles above you will see the light. To develop an accountant mind-set you must always ask yourself "What is behind this transaction?" Indeed, in today's world accounting software do not allow you to understand what is going on behind the scenes. Thereby, once you keep in mind the two principles above, transactions that before you did not understand will suddenly reveal to your eyes. At that point you will understand what I mean when I say that accounting is simple. Once you reach that enlightenment level the whole financial world will unravel to your eyes. Suddenly, this deeper level of understanding will make you love the subject. You will no longer be like a car designer who does not know how the engine works. Therefore, each time the designer has to add a feature to the car skeleton he has to stop and wait for the engineer's approval. To be great in the financial world it is crucial to know the inside out of the accounting books. Like a physicist starts from the relativity theory formula: $e = mc^2$, the accountant starts from the equation: Assets = Liabilities + Equity.

In conclusion, the balance sheet is divided in two main parts. The first part is the one dedicated to Assets. Within it you will find two sub-sections:

- Current Assets
- Long-Term Assets.

On the other hand, the second part is dedicated to liabilities and equity (sources of finance). Within that you will find two sub-sections:

- Liabilities: Current and Non-Current or Long Term Liabilities
- Equity

In the following paragraphs I will explain the two parts separately and then you will see them all together. Before moving on give a look again at the balance sheet template shown at the beginning of the chapter and see if you notice any difference with the Income Statement.

Well, if you looked careful enough you might have noticed that the date of the Balance Sheet is "as of December 31".

Keep in mind the BS is a picture of the business, taken in our example on December 31st. Instead, the P&L is like a collage of pictures taken in the whole year.

Assets: The Future of The Business

The assets side of the Balance Sheet is divided within Current + Non-Current (also called Long-Term Fixed Assets). The current Assets can be defined as the short-term resources of the business. Thereby, they are resources a company can have liquid in less than one accounting cycle. When an organization needs cash to operate the business, the first sources it will look at will be the current assets. The

Non-Current or Long-Term Fixed Assets are investments the company acquired with the intention to keep them on the books for long time. Of course, an organization can still sell or liquidate part of the long-term fixed assets to finance the business, but most of the time this does not happen. Imagine, for example, you need $100,000 to run the operations of your Pizza Store in the next few months. What are you going to do? Are you going to sell the equipment (Long-Term Fixed Asset) that allows you to make the great pizza that drives your sales? Or are you going to ask your customers to pay the outstanding balances (Accounts Receivable-Current Assets) they owe you? Well, if you are a person of common sense you will opt for the second alternative. Indeed, even if you opt for the first one, after selling the equipment that allows you to stay in business you will be bankrupt anyway. Instead, by having your customers pay for their outstanding balance, the organization will have enough resources to survive and more liquidity to thrive in the short-term.

The Assets part of the BS can be divided in:

- *Current Assets:* They are resources an organization has at its disposal and can be easily converted in cash or at least within one operating cycle. The current assets are typically presented from the most liquid to the least liquid.
- *Non-Current or Long-Term Fixed Assets*: They are resources, investments or items kept on company's balance sheet with a long-term perspective. In some cases, the Non-Current Assets are simply long-term investments. In other cases they are functional to the business long-term operations, such as Plants and Equipment. In few cases yet, they are kept on company's books for accounting purposes, such as Goodwill.

At times you may get confused and unsure about the difference between the two. Therefore, ask yourself two basic questions:

What is the Time Frame? Will they be subjected to significant changes in value?

If the answers are: Long-Term (more then one year) and Yes, in the majority of the cases you can be certain to define them as Non-Current Assets.

If instead, your answers are Short-Term (within one year) and No, in the majority of the cases they'll be defined as Current Assets.

Current Assets

• *Cash and Cash Equivalents:* The former includes cash in hand and deposits that can be easily withdrawn. The latter includes short-term highly liquid investments that can be easily liquidated (Converted in cash). Cash Equivalents and Long-Term Investments have two main differences. First the time frame, of course an investment to hold for few years will be not as liquid as a short-term one. On the other hand, the change in value is crucial as well. In fact, Cash Equivalents are usually subject to insignificant changes in value. Instead, Long-Term Investment, reported under Non-Current Assets, can report significant change in value.

- *Accounts Receivable (AR):* They include the amount of money to be received by customers. According to the matching principle (Chapter 1), revenue is reported as soon as realizable. Therefore, the customer did not pay yet for the service already rendered, the money owed will be shown under Accounts Receivable, with heading of Current Assets. The AR can be one of the most difficult accounts on the BS when it comes to quantifying it. Indeed, at times is very complicated to determine the amount of receivable that can be collected.

Example: Imagine you sell raw materials to companies that produce peanut butter. Your customers are companies who have large operations and for such reasons they pay within 90 days from receiving the raw materials. One of your main customers owes you $100K. Its business though is in distress and in few months may be bankrupt. How would you know which percentage of the $100K can be collected? Truth is you won't know until the company will be liquidated and assets sold. Imagine you are able to collect 30% of the outstanding $100K. Overall you recovered $30K. What about the remaining $70K? Well, this will become bad debt. Therefore, you will decrease the AR by 70K and expense this amount as Bad Debt. In conclusion, you understand that AR can be tricky. In few cases the number you see on the BS can be misleading.

- *Inventories:* They can be trickier than the AR when you have to quantify them. Indeed, they are the list of goods a company has on hand to be sold. This definition although is not always true. Imagine the scenario in which you have a company who sells smartphones; nonetheless the production is outsourced. Therefore, your inventories will be mainly comprised of finished product. Imagine the opposite scenario. Your company actually manufactures the smartphones. Therefore, the inventories will be comprised of finished product (smartphones), on one hand, and components on the other hand. As you can imagine the value of the inventories from the first to the second scenario will be slightly different. Inventories will be valued according to the "net realizable value" or the amount for which the goods can be sold for after subtracting the expenses incurred to make the sales. As we saw from the example above, if you own a company who manufactures smartphones, the inventories will be comprised of three kinds of goods that can be valued accordingly:

- *Raw materials.* Typically they include materials that have different values.

Example: Imagine your inventory is comprised of phone screens. With technology progress the price of some components decreases. Therefore, your inventory is comprised of phone screens batches bought one year ago up to three months ago. Further, the batches acquired one year ago are valued at $10 per piece while the newly acquired are valued at $8 per piece. Two methodologies can be used in this case: either the FIFO or the weighted average price. The former means First in, First out. Practically the Inventory will be valued at the price of the latest goods received, in our example $8 per unit. In the latter the price of the goods will be averaged out. For example, the two batches comprise the same number of items, or 50 items at $10 in the first batch and 50 items at $8 in the second batch. Therefore, the weighted average formula will be: ((50 x $8)+(50 x $10))/100 = $9 per unit. In conclusion, according to FIFO the value of your inventory will be $800 or $8 x 100 while according to the weighed average will be $900 or ((50 x $8)+(50 x $10)) x 100).

- *Work in progress.* In the real world these items may be considered worthless. Imagine your inventories are comprised of not fully assembled smartphones, either because the screen is missing or the CPU has not been completed yet. How would you value them from the accounting perspective? Well, do you remember what does the going concern principle state? (Chapter 1). According to this principle accountants assume the business will continue the operations in the foreseeable future. Therefore, in our example the smartphone not fully assembled will be valued more in comparison to the raw materials, since the assumption is that the business will continue the operations long enough to eventually sell the finished product. Furthermore, the value of the work in progress stock will include things such as the labor costs incurred in the manufacturing process. In conclusion, they will have a higher value, although very subjectively determined.

- *Finished goods.* They are the most valuable items of all the inventories. Finished goods can be valued at the net realizable value.

- *Pre-paid Expenses*: Let's define them through an example:

Imagine you own a real estate company. Furthermore, the company bought a 10-story apartment complex. In order for your apartments to be rented of course you have to set up water, trash, gas and electrical accounts. The Utilities Company will ask for a Deposit to set up the accounts. This deposit amount after few months will be credited to your utilities. Therefore, the money paid in advance now will serve you as a credit. This will add short-term liquidity to the business since you already paid for the next few months and you will not need to pay anymore.

Non-Current or Long-Term Fixed Assets

The objective of this paragraph is to show you the classification of Non-Current Assets in few, simple steps. Eventually, you will be able to have a mental image of how they work. I will show you:

Step 1: Difference between OPEX vs. CAPEX.

Step 2: Difference between Tangible and Intangible Assets.

Step 3: Depreciation & Amortization.

Step 1: OPEX vs. CAPEX.

They are the acronyms for Operating Expenditure and Capital Expenditure. For example, imagine you own a real estate firm. The firm bought an apartment complex with few units. In order for you to rent the apartments you have to clean and furnish them. The former activity implies that you call the maid, pay him/her $100 to have the apartment cleaned. The latter activity instead implies buying things, such as: couches, kitchen stoves, beds and so on. They will cost you thousands of dollars but will last for few years. The Operating Expense is money spent on the day-to-day operations of the business. The Capital Expenditure, instead, is money invested in the business with a long-term perspective.

Stop for a second and think. Is the cleaning service OPEX or CAPEX?

The $100 paid to the maid is OPEX. The money spent on furnishing the apartment, instead, will be defined as CAPEX. What helps to discriminate between the two are actually three factors:

- Useful Life (More than one accounting cycle)
- Amount Spent (Over $2,500)
- Future Benefits (Will generate revenue)

Indeed, in the first scenario the maid cleaning expense will have a useful life of few weeks. Furthermore, it is worth less than $2,500 and it won't produce any future benefits. On the other hand, couches and kitchen stoves will have a useful life of few years. Further, whey will be worth over $2,500 and it will produce future benefits. Of course, there are few exceptions.

Example: Imagine, the apartment complex your company bought needs to be repainted. Therefore, the painting work is comprised of: material (Paint) for $500 and labor (Painter) for $5,000. The painter work meets all the criteria above; thereby it is a Capital Expenditure. What about the material (paint)? The paint does not meet all the three CAPEX requirements. Although, it can have a useful life of more than one accounting cycle, in our specific case it is not worth more than $2,500. Indeed, there is no way the painter would be able to finalize the work without paint. Therefore, we will consider the paint as part of the overall work. Thereby, the paint, and the labor will be both considered CAPEX. Why is this difference between operating and capital expenditure crucial?

In reporting terms the operating expense will be stated on the Income Statement (Expense Section), the Capital Expenditure instead will be stated on the Balance Sheet (Non-Current Assets Section).

Why is Capital expenditure stated on the Balance Sheet?

Due to the fact it will be capitalized. What does it mean? Let me give you a further example. Imagine you bought $20,000 worth of furnishing. Assuming that the useful life of the items is ten years. If you were to report the $20K furniture as an expense in the first year your profits would be completely eroded due to the fact that you should report a $20K expense under your income statement. Instead, since this is a capital expenditure it needs to be spread along its useful life. In the specific example: ten years. Thereby, you will report a depreciation expense of $2,000 on your income statement and concurrently decrease the asset value for $2,000 on your balance sheet. See example below:

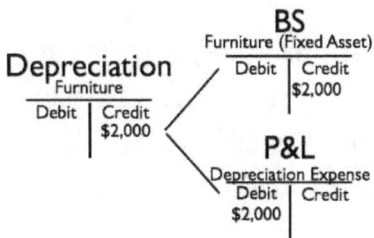

Step 2: The difference between Tangible and Intangible Assets. The former are things with a physical entity, while the latter do not have a physical entity. Imagine you own an IT corporation. What do you need to operate the business? Of course, you need the office, computers and office supplies. Assuming the corporation produces accounting software. How is your organization generating revenue? Through licensing the software. Therefore, it is crucial to make sure no one will clone it.

How can you avoid the cloning? Through patenting the software. In this example, the patent is an Intangible Asset. The remaining assets: Office building, computers and supplies are Tangible Assets.

Why is this difference important?

Step 3: Depreciation & Amortization (D&A).

In the previous example, the IT Corporation needs computers to operate. Assuming 10 computers were bought for $2,000 each, the total Capital Expenditure would be $20K. Furthermore, they won't last forever. Assuming a useful life of five years we have to figure out: What is the depreciation and How to record the transaction.

First, depreciation is the decreasing value of the asset on a yearly basis. Second, the formula to compute the depreciation rate is: (Asset Cost – Residual Value) / Useful Life. Let's solve the previous example: the asset cost of $20,000 minus the residual value of $2,000. Divide the result by 5.

This is the formula: ($20K *Cost* - $2k *Residual Value*) / 5 years *Useful Life*) = $18K / 5 = $3,600 per year. In conclusion, your schedule will look like the following:

Assuming the computers were bought at the beginning of Year 1, at the end of the year their value would decrease by $3,600 at $16,400. Up to Year 5, when the residual value will be $2,000.

	Balance Sheet	Income Statement
End Year 1	$16,400	$3,600
End Year 2	$12,800	$3,600
End Year 3	$9,200	$3,600
End Year 4	$5,600	$3,600
End Year 5	$2,000	$3,600

This method is called straigh-line depreciation. Although there are several depreciation methodologies, the straight-line is the most commonly used.

Why do we need to depreciate? As we saw in *step 1*, it would be unfair to report the whole asset cost under the Income Statement since it would completely erode the Net Income. It is correct instead to spread the value of the asset over the useful life.

Amortization follows the same process of Depreciation. Keep in mind: the tangible assets are depreciated; the intangible assets are amortized. If we go back to the example made a while ago, the IT corporation has at its disposal: tangible assets, such as computers and intangible assets, such as patents. Therefore, the former will be subject to depreciation, the latter to amortization.

Amortization and Depreciation are linked to ordinary events of the assets lives. When, instead, an asset loses value unexpectedly, it will be subject to impairment. Imagine your real estate company bought a building for $10 million, with a useful life of 5 years. At the end of year two due to an earth quick the building is badly damaged. Suddenly the fair market value drops to $5 million. The company decides to sell the building.

How do we estimate the impairment? First, we have to estimate the carrying value of the Building. This is the Cost of the asset minus its accumulated depreciation = $6 million, or $10 million minus $4 million (10 million/5 years = 2 million x 2 years). The book value of the building at year two is $6 million and the recoverable amount is $5 million, therefore the impairment amount is $1 million. The following journal entry will be recorded on our balance sheet and income statement:

The impairment loss will be reported under the P&L as an expense and the accumulated impairment on the BS will decrease the value of the building.

Imagine the opposite scenario. The building increased in fair value instead. At the end of year one, the building is worth $9 million. Given the carrying value of the building of $8 million, it revalued by $1 million. We have to record the revaluation on our books:

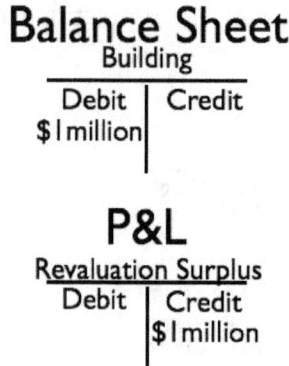

The revaluation will increase the value of the building on the BS and determine a surplus/gain on our P&L.

Liabilities: Too Much Of It Can Get You In Trouble

The liability is an obligation or debt that an organization owes to third parties. On one hand, an organization to operate needs resources such as raw materials in the short-term or capital in the long-term. When the ratio between liabilities on the balance sheet is too high compared to equity, the company is highly leveraged; therefore, more risky. Why is it so? A business can acquire resources through Equity (Its own resources) or Liability (Debt). Equity holders are also called shareholders, and they own part of the organization. In contrast, debt holders are called creditors, and they do not own any part of the organization.

Being a shareholder is advantageous since they get part of the returns generated by the organization. On the other hand, it is a riskier investment, since shareholders are not entitled to ask for repayment of the capital invested and need to cover the losses incurred by the organization.

Being a creditor means not having any of the returns generated by the business, nonetheless creditors get a fixed amount called interest. On the other hand, if the organization declares bankruptcy, the creditors will be the first entitled to repayment. Therefore, creditors can ask for their money back. Furthermore, creditors have "the call to action;" in other words, they can ask to be paid back. Imagine the scenario in which all your creditors ask to be paid back.

What would happen to your business? It will be Bankrupted. Unless you will find enough cash to pay the creditors.

How does an organization generate cash? Through its Assets.

In conclusion a business with higher portion of debt compared to equity is highly leveraged and therefore riskier because its creditors can ask for repayment at any time.

There are several creditors for any organization. In most of the cases companies don't pay right away for the raw materials bought. Indeed, the suppliers may give your organization 60/90 days to pay. This generates a liability for the company. Therefore the suppliers can be defined as short-term creditors.

Consider a second scenario instead. The organization needs $100K to acquire a machine that will drive revenue up in the years to come. To finance the purchase of the machine, a loan is contracted through the Bank. The bank approves the company for a loan to be repaid in ten years. Therefore the Bank will become your creditor. In conclusion there are two kinds of liabilities:

Current Liabilities
They are short-term obligations owed by the organization. They comprise:
- Accounts Payable (AP): money owed to suppliers for goods and services used in day-to-day operations.
- Short-Term Loans and Overdraft. The former can be recalled in the short-term (less than one year), while the latter can be recalled anytime.
- Accrued Expenses. They are the opposite of advanced payments. Indeed, accrued expenses are bills not yet paid; even though service, was already rendered by suppliers.
- Long-Term Liabilities. Obligations/Debt to be paid back in the long-

term. A mortgage can be considered a long-term liability.

Up to this point we covered the part of the balance sheet related to Assets. To wrap up: Assets are comprised of Current and Non-Current Assets. Furthermore, Non-Current Assets are classified as tangible or intangible. Liabilities, instead, are comprised of Current and Long-Term Liabilities. In addition, the equation that drives the BS is: Assets = Liabilities + Equity. Therefore Equity = Assets – Liabilities.

Equity: Strike The Right Balance

While the debt does not give any share or ownership in the business, the equity does. Indeed, equity is the capital to start a venture generating satisfying returns. What can we define as a satisfying or acceptable rate of return? This is hard to assess, since it depends by several variables such as: industry, size, geography and so on. In addition, there are several methodologies to assess the rate of return of an organization, such as: Net Present Value, Internal Rate of Return. In addition, we have other metrics, such as: ROE, ROA and so on. Let's focus in this paragraph on the source of capital, equity and debt. You may be tempted to think that equity is always good for an organization, and the more the better. On one hand, we saw in the previous paragraph, too much debt in proportion to equity can kill the business. In fact, creditors may recall their obligations and this would lead to bankruptcy.

On the other hand, too much equity may be very limiting for a business, although this is not always the case. The capital structure, or how a firm finances its operations and growth by using different sources of funds is crucial. Therefore, a successful organization must be able to use an optimal capital structure, so that debt-equity ratio would maximize the value for its business. For example, in the early 1990s, the private equity industry boomed, due to favorable macroeconomic condition. A disproportionate number of firms with low debt-to-equity ratio formed. In this decade, "LBOs" were very common. The Leveraged buy out is a financial tool that allows private equity firms to acquire or take over organizations, with very minimal amount of equity. Therefore, the perfect targets for private equity firms are listed organizations with far from optimal capital structures, for such reason, undervalued. When private equity firms smell such deals, this becomes a great opportunity to "shop." Further, they borrow money and acquire the firm by pumping up debt and using future cash flows to repay for the contracted obligations. Of course, such increase in debt makes the business riskier, unless it generates enough cash flows to sustain its operations and pay its debt. Therefore, cutting costs and making operations as efficient as possible becomes the motto of the organization. After few years the private equity firms resell the business by making a great return on their investment. In conclusion, having more equity in proportion to debt is a good thing. On the other hand, having too much equity (or operating far from the optimal capital structure), determines undervaluation, therefore vulnerability to hostile take-overs. The last section of the balance sheet is dedicated to equity that is composed by:

Stocks

- Common Stocks: Issued by an organization it helps to finance the business. Who holds common stocks can profit in two ways: Capital Gain, when the value of the stock increases; Paid dividend, when management decides to distribute it.
- Preferred Stocks: Preferred shareholders get paid first and usually in a fixed amount. In many circumstances they do not have voting rights.

Retained profit
Portion of profits retained in the business, instead of being distributed as dividends.

- Reserves.
- Shareholders equity: Total invested capital in the company.

Balancing The Books

At the beginning of the Chapter we saw that the equation Assets = Liabilities + Equity governs the balance sheet. Therefore, it will always be true. When you build your own balance sheet you want to make sure the first sections reconciles with the second.

Example: Imagine you own a Pizza Shop. At the beginning of the year it shows total assets for $250K, of which $100K in total liability and $150K in total Equity. During the year it sold $100K of pizzas and it generated $20K of profits. You decide to retain the earnings instead of distributing the dividends.

How does your balance sheet look like at the end of the year?

First, you have to move the earnings generated throughout the year from your income statement to your balance sheet. Therefore:

| Net Profit | $ 20,000 | | reported as bottom line of the P&ℓ |
| Retained Earnings | | $ 20,000 | reported on Equity Section of the |

Eventually the balance sheet will show total assets for $270K of which $100K in total liability and $170K in total equity:

Balance Sheet	Year Start	Year End
Total Assets	250,000	270,000
Total liability	100,000	100,000
Total Equity	150,000	170,000

When your assets increase, accordingly either your liability or equity will concomitantly increase.

Chapter 7. The Cash Flow Statement

"The fact is that one of the earliest lessons I learned in business was that balance sheet and income statements are fiction, cash flow is reality" **Chris Chocola** (Credit: BrainyQuote)

The cash flow statement is the third main statement. Together with P&L and BS, helps to assess the health of any organization. As we saw in the previous chapter, the Profit and Loss focuses on return while the BS on risk. The cash flow statement focuses on cash. There are two methods to present the cash flow: direct and indirect. In this chapter we will focus on the latter, since it is the most commonly used. In addition, it allows the reconciliation of the Net Income with the cash provided by operations, investments and financing activities. To build a CFS with the indirect method, we start from the Net Profit (P&L), adjust it according to the BS. You will see in the cash flow from operations the reason why we start from net profit. For now let me tell you the story of a friend of mine: James.

Cash Is King

This is true in life but particularly true in business. Keep in mind that there are three main activities, which generate cash: operating, financing and investing. Let me tell you the story of a friend of mine, we will call him "James." He used to run a successful restaurant. Indeed, he was in business for over ten years now. Every night he had hundreds of customers and everyone knew him in town. He was named restaurateur of the year. The future seemed so bright. In fact, he believed that having popular customers made his business grow faster or at least made it more popular. Therefore, half of his clientele was comprised of popular people in town. Many of them went to his restaurant and after bringing other people along, James allowed them to do so. He allowed to other prestigious customers to open credit accounts called "VIP Accounts." Therefore, they could come at any time and pay whenever they were able to. Initially, this seemed to work. More regular customers came in and his profits skyrocketed. Although, business had never been so good, he was short of cash. Furthermore, salaries for half of the staff were not paid. The staff loved James and they were willing to stay few weeks more without getting paid but they expected him to pay within three weeks. Taken aback he went to the bank and asked for a Loan. Once there, the director of the bank, a long time friend of him wanted to help him but he couldn't. Even though the business looked successful from the outside, it was bleeding from the inside. Cash was short; nonetheless the restaurant produced $50K in profits, there was a $20K hole due to unpaid balances by customers. In fact, the account receivable showed over $200K due, 75% of it were over two years old balance. The bank director told James if he wanted to borrow money he had to improve the cash situation. Therefore, he turned to his managers and asked them to use any methods to collect the money lumped as accounts receivable. The AR skyrocketed in the last two years mainly due to the "VIP accounts." Lately the restaurant managers were trying to collect the balances from the customers and in some cases by threatening them. The VIP accounts holders felt offended. Therefore, they decided to avoid James' restaurant and not to pay their balances. Their understanding was that James offered them food in exchange for marketing services. Not only James lost the chance to collect the money lumped in the AR, but half of the clientele was gone. Further, his employees decided to leave. James did not see any other solution that closing the business and declaring bankruptcy. The hole went from $20K to over $200K!

What seemed to be a successful venture and what seemed to be a small cash issue, turned out to be bankrupt. This was mainly due to poor cash management.

THE THREE MAIN SOURCES OF CASH

What are the main sources of cash for a business? Let's go back to James' story. Initially, he had a hole of $20K due to the fact that its restaurant operations were not generating enough cash. Therefore, he went to the bank to find cash to *finance* the business but he was turned down. Eventually, what killed the business was a total lack of *investments* in long-term assets, since James spent hundreds of thousands of dollars in marketing, with no focus whatsoever on employees or new equipment. This is how a CFS would look like:

Operating Activities
Net Income
Adjustments for non-cash items
+ Depreciation & Amortization
+ Deferred Income Taxes
+ Deferred & Unearned Compensation
Δ **Working Capital**
Total Operating Activities

Investing Activities
Δ CAPEX
Net Cash from Investing Activities

Financing Activities
Δ Notes Payable
Δ Short-term debt
Δ Long-term debt
Δ Bonds Payable
Δ Common Stock
Δ Retained Earnings
Net Cash from Financing Activities

As shown in the picture above, the first section is related to operations, then investing activities, eventually financing activities. Before moving on to the cash flow from operations let me clarify one thing. Indeed, if you look at the CFS picture, you will notice a small sign "Δ" called Delta. This is the fourth letter of the ancient Greek alphabet. In our particular case Δ means change or incremental value. Indeed, the P&L and BS items are reported in absolute values. For example, if you look at the P&L, the reported revenue will refer to the entire year. Instead, in the cash flow statement each item is considered from an incremental value standpoint. If you report the accounts receivable, you will take the difference between the current-year, over the previous year. For example, in Year Two, you have $100 of AR while in Year One you had $50. This implies that your AR grew of $50 from Year One to Year Two. So the delta is the difference between Year Two and Year One, or $50. But what happened from the cash standpoint? Let me explain in the next paragraph.

Cash Inflow versus Cash Outflow

In order for you to fully understand the cash flow statement you have to change perspective. Indeed, so far we looked at the P&L and BS through the accrual basis lenses. It is time now to shift your perspective to the cash basis. What does it mean? Well, let's look again at the example, from the previous paragraph. Our accounts receivable went from

$50 in Year One to $100 in Year Two. From the accrual standpoint, it means an increase in asset. But what if we change perspective and we look at it from the cash standpoint? Well, from the cash standpoint means a cash outflow! What? Why? The reason is simple. The purpose of the CFS is to look at cash inflows and outflows for a certain time frame with no regard to profits generated. In fact, in the next paragraph I will show you why the net profit is a liar. For now, keep in mind that an Asset increase means a cash outflow, while an Asset decrease means a cash inflow. Instead, a Liability increase means a cash inflow, while a Liability decrease a cash outflow. The Cash Flow matrix below will help you remember this basic assumption:

From the previous example, the increase in asset (AR) from Year-Two to Year-One determined a cash outflow of $50. See below:

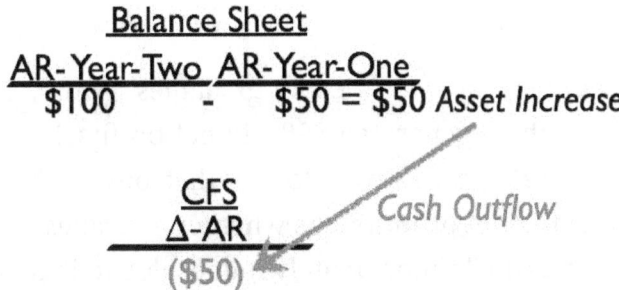

To recapitulate we saw that the cash flow statement takes into account the incremental values, called "Δ" (Delta) and that from the cash standpoint an increase in assets determine a cash outflow, and vice-versa, while an increase in liabilities determine a cash inflow, and vice-versa.

Why is the Net Profit a liar?

Balance Sheet Items	Cash Inflow +	Cash Outflow −
Assets	↓	↑
Liabilities	↑	↓

- Assets decrease you will have a cash inflow. Assets increase you will have a cash outflow.
- Liabilities increase you will have a cash inflow. Liabilities decrease you will have a cash outflow.

The Net Profit Is a Liar

Let's take a step back to James' story. Although he generated $50K in net profits, he had a $20K cash hole. How is that possible? Shouldn't net profit tell us whether a business is successful? Unfortunately it doesn't and it is actually possible to see organizations with positive net income, eventually going bankrupt because of lack of short-term liquidity. James had a small business and he knew how to look at the Income Statement but none taught him how to manage the cash or read a CFS. The net profit of course is a measure of profitability, but what does profitability mean? An organization is profitable when its revenues cover its total expenses, as we saw in *chapter 5.* Does revenue or expense mean cash received or disbursed? No, it doesn't. In *chapter 5,* we saw that according to the matching principle, the revenue and expense are recognized as soon as realizable, and not realized. What is the difference between realizable and realized? The latter means that a product or service is offered in exchange for cash. The former, instead, means that products are delivered and services performed. Therefore, the net profit does not give any information about cash. Indeed, the purpose of the CFS in general is to adjust the Net Income, to reflect all cash inflows and outflows happened for a certain period.

Cash Flow From Operations: Are We Efficient?

In this paragraph we will see how to build a cash flow from operations, using the P&L and Balance Sheet. The main purpose of this statement is to take off from the net income the non-cash items included in it and all the cash inflows and outflows that happened in a certain period. Let's look at the image below:

Operating Activities
Net Income
Adjustments for non-cash items
+ Depreciation & Amortization
+ Deferred Income Taxes
+ Deferred & Unearned Compensation
Δ **Working Capital**
Total Operating Activities

The net income is the starting point. Why do we start from the Net Income? Let me clarify again. The Net Income is given by Revenue – Expense. When revenues or expenses are generated, it does not mean cash was generated. By going back to James' restaurant example, a profit of $50K for the year generated a hole of $20K. Why? Well, in the specific case, most of the income reported as revenue was comprised of receivables, which were not collected for over two years. Therefore, the purpose of the cash flow is to clean the net income from all these non-cash items and non-cash expenditure comprised in it. Let me show you now the three simple steps to build your cash flow from operations:

Step 1: Find the non-cash items: In fact, they did not contribute any cash inflow or outflow. Therefore, before we clean the net income from these items, let's find them:

- *Depreciation & Amortization expense:* The former is the recorded decline in value of assets. The latter is the distribution of cost for intangible assets. On one hand, they were reported as expenses in the P&L and they affected negatively the NI. Indeed, the Depreciation expense allows businesses to reduce their Profit Before Tax and by doing so, reducing their taxable income. On the other hand, the depreciation expense did not determine any cash outflow. Thereby D&A need to be added back to the NI.

- *Impairment:* When an asset loses value significantly and abruptly, we have impairment. It happens when the carrying amount exceeds the recoverable amount. Although, it affects the Net Income negatively, since it will be reported as expense, under the P&L, it does not imply any cash outflow. Therefore, it needs to be added back to the NI.

- *Profit/Loss on sale of non-current assets:* When a non-current asset is sold, the profit/loss generated is recognized under the P&L and it will affect the net income. However, at this stage is too early to recognize the sale of the non-current asset, since this will be taken into account in the cash flow from investments. Therefore, to avoid any double counting this item will be subtracted in the OCF and added back in the Cash flow from investing.

- *Increase/Decrease in inventory, receivable and payables:* These three items taken into account altogether form the "working capital". Defined as the resources an organization has at its disposal used to sustain the operations in the short-term; the formula for the Working capital is given by: Current Assets – Current Liabilities. In the cash flow statement though we take into account the Δ in working capital or change in working capital. This means the incremental value reported as result of the Incremental Inventory + Incremental Receivable + Incremental Payable.

Step 2: Take the Net Income and add back all non-cash items. How these items affect the cash? Let me give you an example on each item. Imagine, your restaurant business reported a net income at the end of Year-Two for $300,000, let us see how to adjust the net income to get the cash flow from operations:

• *Depreciation effect on cash:* At the beginning of Year-One you bought the kitchen equipment. The whole cost was $100,000 and it will have a useful life of ten years and a residual value of $5,000. The depreciation expense in Year-Two is $9,500 or ($100,000 - $5,000)/10. Therefore, at the end of Year-Two an expense for $9,500 will be included as

Depreciation expense in the P&L. We have to add it back for two main reasons: First the depreciation expense implies no cash outflow. Second, we will take into account the change in non-current assets through the cash flow from investments. In conclusion, we take the $300,000 earnings for Year-Two and add back $9,500 of depreciation expense (non-cash expense) = $309,500.

- *Profit/loss on sale of non-current assets' effect on cash:* In Year-One you bought a machine to produce fresh pasta. You paid $3,000 for the machine and the estimated useful life is three years with no residual value at the end. The depreciation rate is $1,000 or $3,000/3. In Year-Two the machine is reported as worth $2,000 on your BS, since you depreciated it by 1/3 or $1,000. You eventually sell it for $2,500. It means a profit of $500 ($2,500, *selling price* - $2,000 *asset value per BS*). The profit from the sale, $500 is included already in the NI in Year-Two. We have to take them out for two reasons. First, although there is a profit of $500, this is just a "paper profit" (In the real world the machine was bought for $3,000 and sold for $2,500).

Second, the Profit/Loss coming from the sale of non-current assets will be taken into account in the Cash flow from investment. Therefore, to avoid any double counting it is crucial to take it out from the OCF. Going back to the example, recall in the previous bullet point we added back the depreciation expense from the NI and we had $309,500. Furthermore, Let's take off the "paper profit" generated by the machine sales. Therefore, $309,500 - $500 = $309,000.

- *Net Working Capital effect on cash:* As we said in *step 1*, the net working capital is given by: Incremental AR + Incremental Inventory + Incremental Payable. Let's assume in Year-One you had $500,000 in AR, $240,000 in Inventory and $300,000 in AP. In Year-Two, instead, you have respectively $550,000, $200,000, and $350,000. See below how to translate the net working capital from the balance sheet to the OCF:

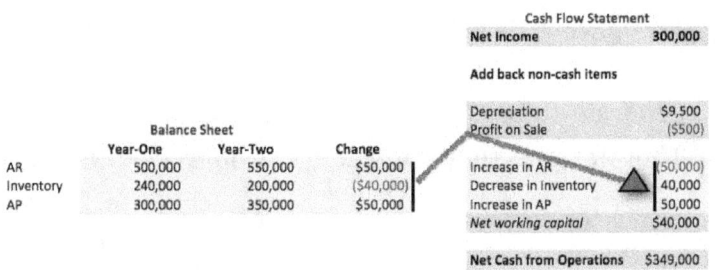

Notice the increase in AR from Year-One to Year-Two determined a decrease in cash. A decrease in Inventory determined an increase in cash and an increase in AP determined an increase in cash. Therefore, the Net working capital is $40,000, that adds up to $309,000. Eventually, we get $349,000.

Although, the NI for Year-Two was $300,000 the Net OCF was $349,000.

Cash Flow From Investing: Are We Killing The Goose?

In this section are shown the cash inflows/outflows related to non-current assets, such as property, plant and equipment. The non-current assets are the ones that generate future benefits for the organization. Therefore, they are considered as investments. In *Chapter 6*, we saw the difference between CAPEX and OPEX. Indeed, all the money spent on acquiring things that will have a useful life over one year at least, worth more than $2,500 and that will bring future benefits to the organization can be defined as CAPEX. In this category are included all non-current assets under the balance sheet, such as: property, plant and equipment. In the previous paragraph, we saw that to avoid double counting, items such as depreciation & amortization, sales of non-current assets are added back to the NI to get the OCF. Some examples of cash flows generated from investing activities are:

- Disposal or Purchase of fixed assets
- Disposal or Purchase to buy shares or interest in other joint ventures

If we go back of the example from the previous paragraph, so far the cash generated by operating activities is $349,000. Furthermore, we want to see the cash flows generated by the investing activities. For example, imagine, at the beginning of Year-Two you decide to renovate the building owned by the restaurant business. The building is worth $300,000 on your balance sheet. The renovation costs you $50,000 and it lasts few months. The money spent in renovating the building is not operating expenses. Therefore, they can be defined as capital expenditure since they increase the value of the building on the balance sheet. From the cash standpoint this means a cash outflow of $50,000. The cash flow will look like the following:

As you can see from the image above, the $50,000 spent to improve the building will determine a cash outflow for the same amount. Therefore, CAPEX will be (50,000), that will reduce the cash generated in Year-Two.

Cash Flow Statement

Net Income	**300,000**
Add back non-cash items	
Depreciation	$9,500
Profit on Sale	($500)
Increase in AR	(50,000)
Decrease in Inventory	40,000
Increase in AP	50,000
Net working capital	$40,000
Net Cash from Operations	**$349,000**
Cash from investing	
CAPEX	(50,000)

Balance Sheet

	Beginning Year-Two	End Year-Two
Building	300,000	300,000
Building Improvements		50,000
Total Building	300,000	350,000

Cash Flow From Financing: The Cash Paradox

This is the cash generated through activities focused on raising money for the long-term growth of the business. In *Chapter 6*, we saw how important is for any business to find the resources to boost income in the long run. Indeed, too much debt can be lethal, while a business not able to issue debt through banks or other creditors may be a bad signal as well. In fact, when a business is lacking the credibility or trust of the markets, no one will lend money to it. For such reason, although raising debt translates to long-term liabilities and higher risk for the business, finding the optimal capital structure is crucial for any organizations.

Cash Flow Statement	
Net Income	300,000
Add back non-cash items	
Depreciation	$9,500
Profit on Sale	($500)
Increase in AR	(50,000)
Decrease in Inventory	40,000
Increase in AP	50,000
Net working capital	$40,000
Net Cash from Operations	$349,000
Cash from Investing	
CAPEX	(50,000)
Cash from Financing	
Note Payable to Partner	(50,000)

Balance Sheet			
	Year-One	Year-Two	Delta
Note Payable to Partner	100,000	50,000	(50,000)

There is no magic rule for it. And it really depends on the kind of business you are operating. Of course, if you own a manufacturing company, it will need much more resources to run the operations, since it is much more capital intensive. Therefore, this implies a higher debt equity ratio, without making the business necessarily riskier, given its more stable income streams. On the other hand, if you own a service or IT organization, you don't need much capital to run the operations and given the highly competitive industry, you will report unstable income streams. This makes the business more risky in its own right. Therefore, it is better to have a lower debt to equity ratio. Not by chance, companies such as Apple and Microsoft keep high cash reserves. Indeed, a manufacturing company in a traditional industry has more chances to survive for decades. An IT organization has less chance to pass two decades of life. To go back to our previous example, remember that you bought the kitchen equipment for $100,000, in Year-One. You found the resources to buy them through one of your partners who loaned the money to the restaurant business to be repaid in three years. At the end of Year-One you don't make any payment, but at the end of Year-Two you decide the pay half of the debt. This means you will report a cash outflow of $50,000. When liabilities decrease, they determine a cash outflow, since the debit is getting repaid and you are using cash to pay it back. Eventually, our cash flow will look like the following:

Cash Flow Statement	
Net Income	**300,000**
Add back non-cash items	
Depreciation	$9,500
Profit on Sale	($500)
Increase in AR	(50,000)
Decrease in Inventory	40,000
Increase in AP	50,000
Net working capital	$40,000
Net Cash from Operations	**$349,000**
Cash from investing	
CAPEX	(50,000)
Cash from Financing	
Note Payable to Partner	(50,000)
Net Cash for the Period	**$249,000**

At the end of Year-Two, although a NI of $300,000, the net cash for the period was $249,000, while the cash from operations was

$349,000. Due to an increase in net working capital, given by decreased inventory, that means the company sold more goods that it has purchased. This had a beneficial effect on cash that generated a cash inflow for $40,000. Further, an increase in AP determines a cash inflow as well. This is due to new credit condition given by suppliers. They allowed you to have more time to pay for the purchased goods or raw materials. When a business is able to play on the time difference between AR and AP it creates liquidity to run the business. Let me explain trough an example. Imagine, you own a business and you sell canned tomatoes. You do not produce them, since the product is bought from other tomato factories. Therefore, after getting the canned tomato from the manufacturer, you label it and sell it to final customers. Thereby, the tomato factory is your supplier, while the retailers are your customers. Thanks to the long-term friendship with the manufacturers you are able to secure payments every sixty days. On the other hand, your customers pay you every thirty days. Imagine, you place the first order of canned tomatoes for $100 and you will repay them in sixty days. In the same day, the canned tomatoes are labeled and sold to customers. They pay you $2 per piece and buy 100 pieces. At the end of the first month you generated $200 in revenue and one additional month to pay your suppliers. Therefore, in one month you generated $100 of additional profits financed by your customers. Companies which are able to tight the AR while stretching the AP can generate additional liquidity for the organization, with no additional cost.

Book Conclusions

At the beginning of the 20th century in the U.S., the mob phenomenon exploded. One of the most powerful exponents was Al Capone. He ranked among the most despicable gangsters of all time. He killed dozens of people. The climax came in 1929, when he ordered the assassinations of seven rivals. This became the greatest massacre in mob history. How did the story of Al Capone story end? Although he committed thousands of crimes he was only convicted with one. In 1931, he was finally convicted for Tax Evasion. A pool of Forensic Accountants directed the investigation. He served in prison for almost seven years. After that Al Capone was debilitated and mentally ill, he had to renounce to his mob career. Accountants were the ones that brought down Al Capone. While you may never bring criminals to justice through your accounting, you can realize the power that accounting does have.

Although becoming a good accountant is a path that might take years of experience, forming the Accountant mindset is instead something that anyone can start at any time. Understanding and becoming aware of the fact that Accounting is the foundation of business is a crucial step to take. The "Enlightened Accountant" gave you the tools to start this path. Begin now to analyze the world with the Accountant eye. There are many actions that anyone takes each day, such as: going to the barber shop, the bakery, having a coffee with a friend, going out for dinner and paying with the credit card, borrowing money from a friend, lending money to a friend. In all these circumstances ask yourself: "How would this transaction look like in the Accounting world?" Of course it might be that you do not want to undertake a career as Accountant or CPA, although you have to understand what goes behind the 14 trillion transactions that happen each day in U.S. alone. In addition, you have to aspire to become an "Enlightened Accountant". The difference between the Accountant and the Enlightened Accountant stands in the way they look at the world. The former, although, has a deep technical knowledge of the subject remains unaware of the big picture. The Enlightened Accountant instead is the one who understands how the Accounting world intertwines with the business world. When I first started to work as an Assistant Controller I did not appreciate the importance of it, until I realized that Accounting gave me the lenses through which I could look at the business world with more clarity.

About The Author

Gennaro Cuofano International MBA. He has been working in the international management field, across Europe and US in the last ten years. He loves educating and helping students and practitioners succeed in the career path of their dreams.

Connect with Gennaro:

Icon credit: iconfinder

Consult other books by Gennaro Cuofano

$2.99
Kindle Edition

$9.99
Paperback

$2.99
Kindle Edition

$2.99
Kindle Edition

Online Courses

Get any course for 50% off! Use the code **"newskill"** at www.udemy.com/user/gennarocuofano

Financial Analysis from Scratch to Professional Level
Become Financial Analyst, We help people in boosting their...
★★★★★ (4)
$20

Awaken the Accountant in You | Master the Accounting...
Become Financial Analyst, We help people in boosting their...
★★★★★ (4)
$20

How to Become an Accountant from scratch!
Become Financial Analyst, We help people in boosting their...
★★★★★ (8)
$20

How to Become a Financial Analyst from Scratch!
Become Financial Analyst, We help people in boosting their...
★★★★★ (21)
$20

Additional Suggested Reading

Accounting in a Nutshell, Third Edition:
Accounting for non-specialist, Janet Walker

Double-Entry: How the Merchants of Venice created Modern Finance, Jane Gleeson-White

Useful Websites

- www.investopedia.com
- www.accountingcoach.com
- www.businessdictionary.com
- www.becomefinancialanalyst.com
- www.fourweekmba.com

www.ingramcontent.com/pod-product-compliance
Lightning Source LLC
Chambersburg PA
CBHW060354190526
45169CB00002B/593